Creative Crafts

Make-up Art

Ron Freeman

Consultant: Henry Pluckrose

Photography: Chris Fairclough

W

FRANKLIN WATTS

LONDON • SYDNEY

This edition 2005

Franklin Watts
96 Leonard Street
London EC2A 4XD

Franklin Watts Australia
Level 17/207 Kent Street
Sydney, NSW 2000

ISBN: 0 7496 6413 4

Hardback edition published
in the Fresh Start series.

Design: K and Co
Editor: Jenny Wood
Typeset by Lineage Ltd,
Watford, England

Printed in Belgium

Acknowledgement
The author and publisher would
like to thank the following young
people who have been used in the
illustrations: Amy Lynn; Stefan
Radwanski; Danny Sweetman;
Emma Tingle.

Contents

Equipment and materials

This book describes activities which use the following:

Brushes (sable and moppet, see page 5. These brushes are best, but cheaper brushes can be used)
Chair
Cotton wool
Crêpe hair
Diamanté tears
Eyebrow pencils
Eyelash glue
'Kryolan' hairspray (coloured)
Mirror (large)
Mixing palette
Newspaper
Paper tissues
Paper towels
Pencils (and colouring pencils for initial designs)
Pre-impression caps

Rouge
Rubbish bin
Scissors
Sheets (old, for covering model and table)
Sketch pad (for initial designs)
Soap (for washing hands/face)
Sponges
Spirit gum
Spirit gum remover
Table
Theatrical make-up colours: – Kryolan (Aqua Colour)
– Star Gazer
Toothbrush
Towels
Water
Water pot/jar

Keep your make-up in a strong box.

1 Make-up, a basic kit.

This book has been written to encourage you to experiment with colours which can safely be used, at home or at school, to 'make up' the face. Whether you want to disguise yourself at a fancy dress party or you are thinking of taking part in a drama production at school or at your youth club, the pages which follow will teach you how to use water-based colours to change your appearance – and that of your friends!

A number of different make-ups are featured. Each illustrates the processes you will need to master. Although the processes are important, you do not need to follow the designs exactly. Being creative is not just following instructions! The creative person takes an idea, experiments, and in so doing achieves something which is his or her own.

Equipment

All the colours described in this book are water-based. They can be applied on a damp sponge, or with a brush. 'Kryolan' colours can be bought from any shop which sells theatrical make-up, and are sold singly or in boxed sets. For beginners, I suggest that a basic set, containing a range of colours, is the best buy. You will also need some cakes of 'Aqua Colour'. These are essential for preparing a base on which to work and are available in a range of colours. 'Star Gazer' colours are useful for adding fine detail.

Several types of brushes are used in make-up. You will need some sable brushes (Sizes 6, 8 and 10) and some moppet brushes. A moppet brush has a large, soft head. In your make-up kit you will require a 1.2cm round-headed moppet brush and a 1.2cm chisel-headed moppet brush.

In many designs, it will be necessary to conceal the model's hair. This is easily achieved by using a pre-impression cap (also available from shops which sell theatrical make-up). The cap is held in position with spirit gum.

Some hints

Applying make-up can be back-breaking work. Make sure that your model (the person who is to be made up) sits on a chair with a high seat. Raise your model if necessary by putting a thick, firm cushion (or even a box) on the seat of the make-up chair.

Remember, your model will need to be comfortable. Make-up cannot be applied quickly and the model may have to sit still for quite a long time.

1 Place a table in front of the make-up chair. Set out on the table all the materials you will need. Your make-up mirror should also stand on the table.

2 The mirror is an essential piece of equipment. When you make up a model you will need to glance continuously into the mirror to see how your design is developing, to make sure that the features on each side of the face balance and that the colours are evenly applied.

3 The table arranged for working.

Like most craft activities, applying face make-up can be a little messy. Be prepared for mess before you make it. Use an old sheet or cloth to cover the table. Place a bin near the make-up chair, for waste material. The model will need covering, too – a sheet or towel over his or her shoulders will be sufficient. When not using a pre-impression cap, keep the model's hair off his or her face with a stocking or hairband.

The water-based make-up used in the examples which follow is easy to remove, but you will have to make sure that you have access to soap, towels and a ready supply of hot water. If moustaches and beards are part of the make-up, you will also require spirit gum remover. Never apply make-up if there is no way of removing it safely and easily. Cleansing is essential.

Finally, before you begin to work on a model, be sure that you know the design you are to follow. Always begin with a sketch. Some of the drawings prepared for the designs in this book are included in the text.

A doll

You will need a sponge, 'Aqua Colour' shade 4W, 'Star Gazer' colour blue, sable brushes, rouge powder, a moppet brush, black and red 'Kryolan' colours, and an eyebrow pencil.

1 A sketch of the design.

2 Dampen the sponge and use it to apply 'Aqua Colour' (shade 4W) to the face and the neck to just below the costume line.

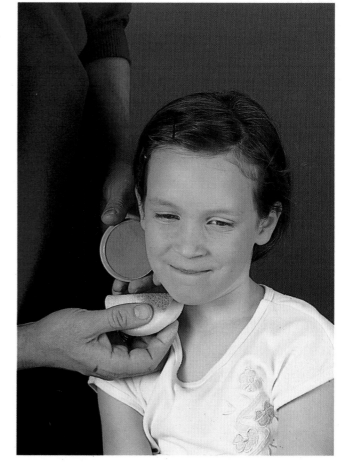

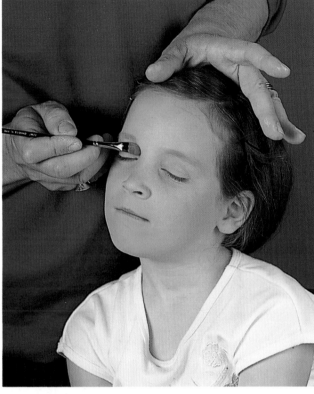

3 Now make up the eyelids using 'Star Gazer' colour blue.

4 Apply rouge to the cheeks with the moppet brush.

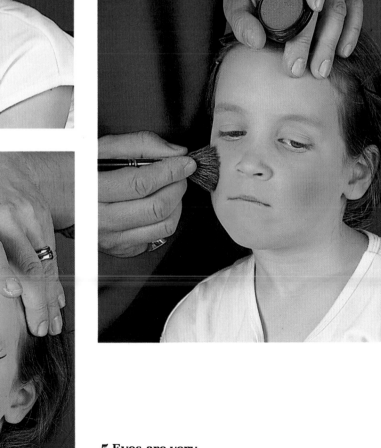

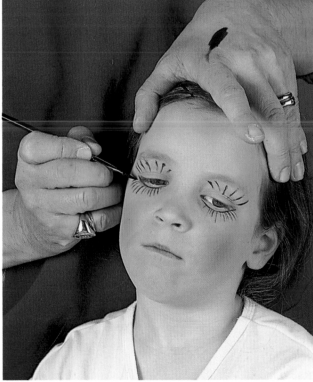

5 Eyes are very important features in all face make-up. Black 'Kryolan' emphasises the eye line...

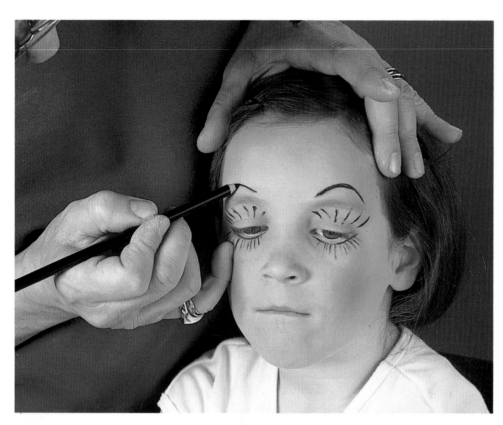

6 ... and the eyebrow pencil is used to strengthen the eyebrows.

7 Finally, paint the lips with red 'Kryolan'.

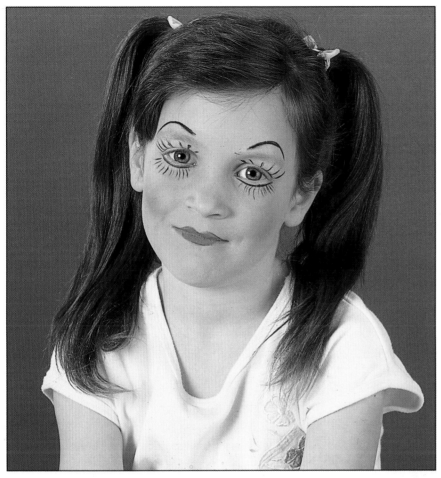

8 *The Doll.* Compare the finished result with the original sketch...

9 ... and with this photograph of Amy, the model.

You will need a pre-impression cap, scissors, spirit gum, sponges, white 'Aqua Colour', 'Kryolan' colours in various shades according to your design, and sable brushes (Size 6).

1 A sketch of the design.

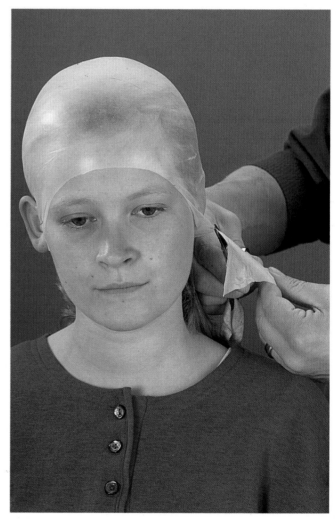

2 For this design, the model's hair must be taken away from the face using the pre-impression cap. The cap is cut away around the eyes, and slots are made for the ears. Apply spirit gum around the edges of the cap to hold it in position on the head. Press with a damp sponge or wet towel. Don't use your fingers!

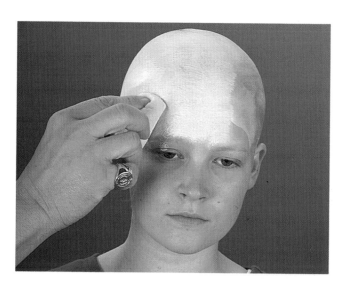

3 Using a damp sponge, apply white 'Aqua Colour' evenly around the join by dabbing...

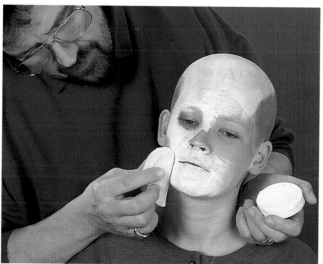

4 ... all over the face, ...

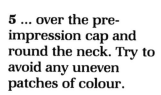

5 ... over the pre-impression cap and round the neck. Try to avoid any uneven patches of colour.

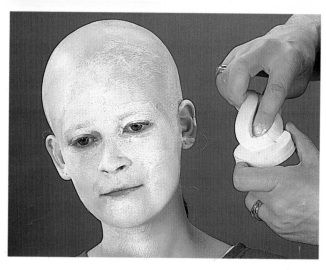

6 Now decorate the face with 'Kryolan' colours applied by brush. Work from the eyes outwards. Look in the mirror to make sure that the design is identical on both sides of the face.

7 The advantage of 'Kryolan' colours is that you can work one colour after the other without waiting for the first colour to dry. If you make a mistake, just wipe off the paint and start again. Sometimes the 'mistakes' can be made into part of your design!

8 Colour the lips.

9 The completed design. Compare the finished result with the original sketch...

10 ... and with this photograph of Emma, the model.

You will need a pre-impression cap, scissors, spirit gum, a damp sponge, black, red and white 'Kryolan' colours, and sable brushes.

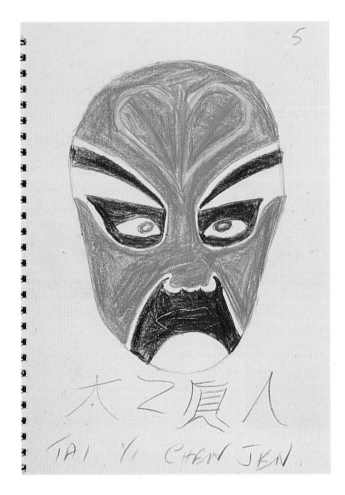

1 A sketch of the design.

2 Cover the hair with the pre-impression cap. Shape it around the ears and fix it in position with spirit gum. (See page 12.)

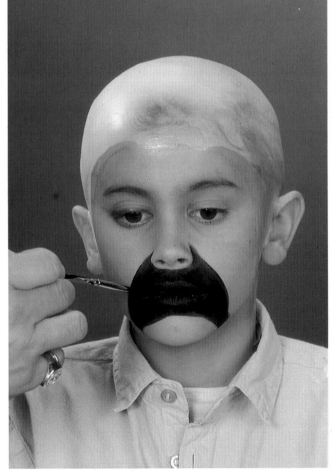

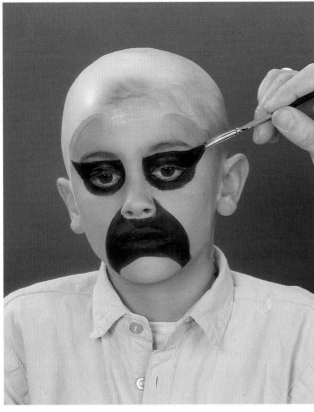

3 Colour the mouth and eyes with black 'Kryolan'.

4 Whiten the chin, nostrils and the area around the eyes.

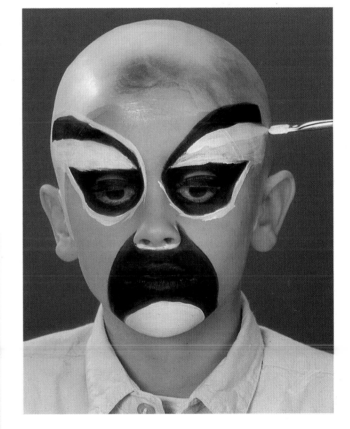

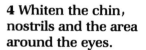

5 Cover the rest of the face with red 'Kryolan', using a brush.

6 The completed design. Compare the finished result with the original sketch...

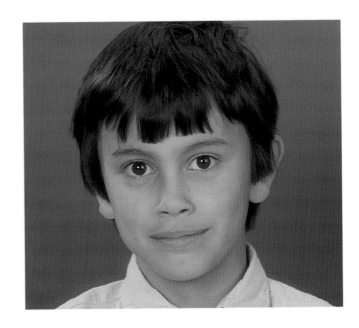

7 ... and with this photograph of Danny, the model.

This design does not require a sketch. You will need a pre-impression cap, spirit gum, sponges, gold and black Aqua Colour, and a sable brush.

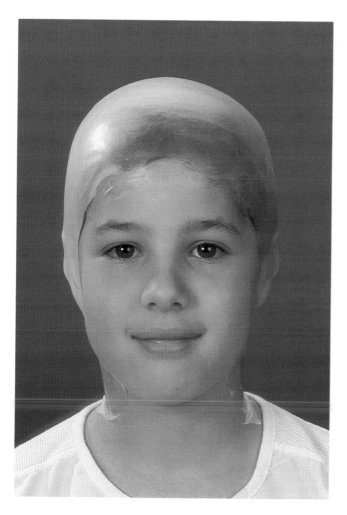

1 Begin by covering the hair and ears with the pre-impression cap. Fix it in position with spirit gum (see page 12).

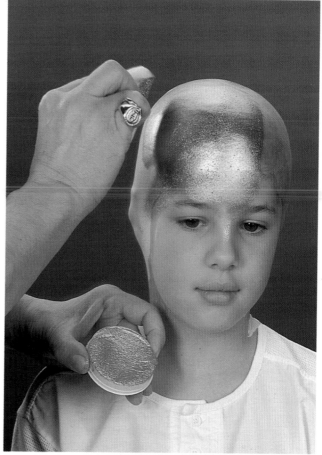

2 Now apply gold 'Aqua Colour' all over the head, face...

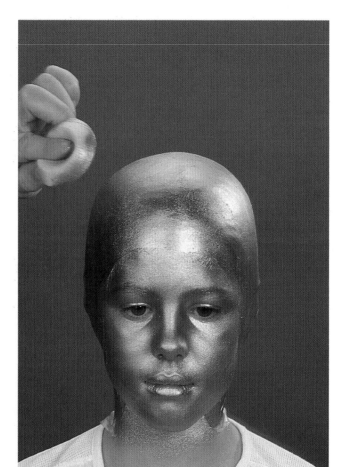

3 ... and neck, using a damp sponge.

4 Final details around the nostrils and eyes are added in black 'Kryolan', applied by brush. Experiment with your own robot make-up ideas.

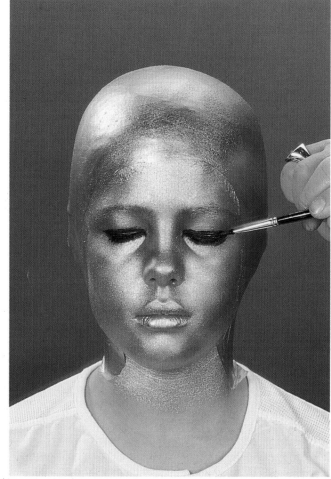

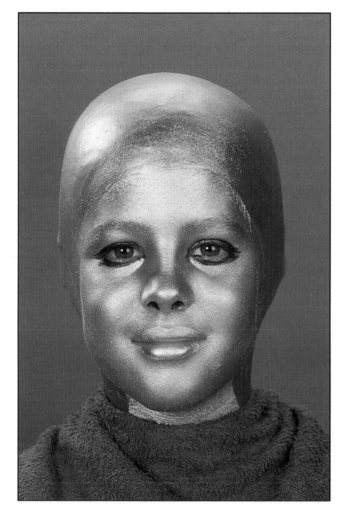

5 The completed design.

6 Compare the finished result with this photograph of Stefan, the model.

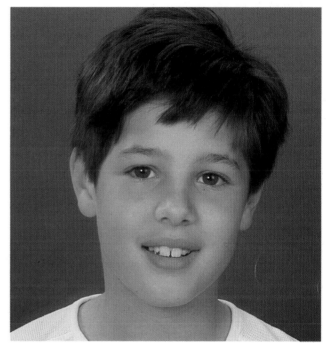

7 Many strange creatures can be found in the studios of a theatrical make-up artist!

This is a traditional design and a sketch should not be necessary. You will need a pre-impression cap, scissors, spirit gum, sponges, white 'Aqua Colour', black and red 'Kryolan' colours, sable brushes, a diamanté tear and eyelash glue.

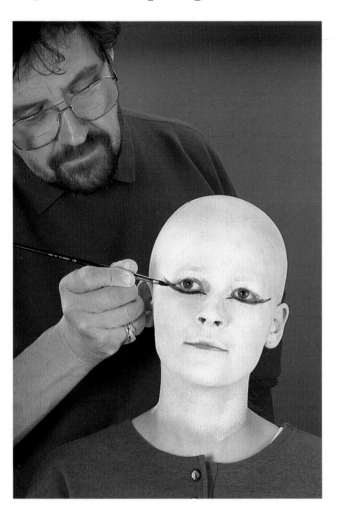

1 Cover the hair with the pre-impression cap. Shape it around the ears and fix it in position with spirit gum. (See page 12.) Now cover the face and cap with a layer of white 'Aqua Colour' applied by dabbing with a damp sponge. Outline the eyes with black 'Kryolan'.

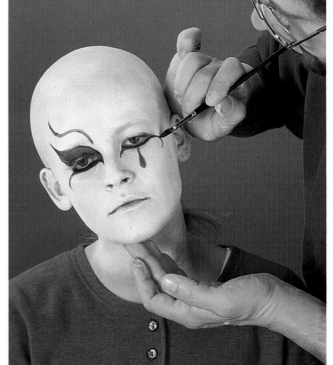

2 Add more black 'Kryolan' around the eyes, and add a dark tear-drop.

3 Use the black 'Kryolan' to emphasise the line of the lips, too.

4 Colour the lips with red 'Kryolan'.

5 Add the diamanté tear last of all. Coat the back of the tear lightly with eyelash glue and stick it on the cheek.

A punk

You will need a pre-impression cap, spirit gum, sponges, grey, purple, lilac and black 'Kryolan' colours, a palette, water, a 1.2cm flat-headed sable brush, a lip brush, an eyebrow pencil, a length of crêpe hair, a sheet of newspaper, and 'Kryolan' hairspray.

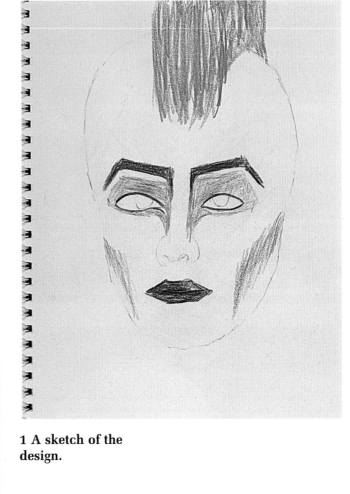

1 A sketch of the design.

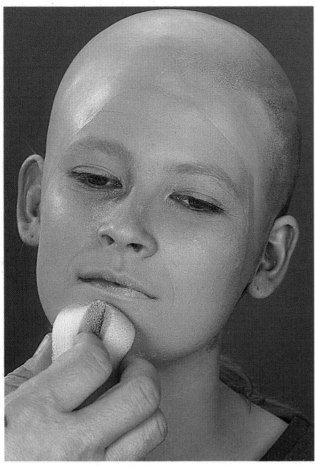

2 Cover the hair with the pre-impression cap. Shape it around the ears and fix it in position with spirit gum. (See page 12.) Apply grey 'Kryolan' over the cap and the face, using a damp sponge.

3 The eye colour was made by mixing together purple and lilac 'Kryolan'. Put some of each colour on to the palette, add a little water and mix the colours together. Add more purple or lilac as required, to obtain the exact shade. Use the sable brush to apply the eye colour.

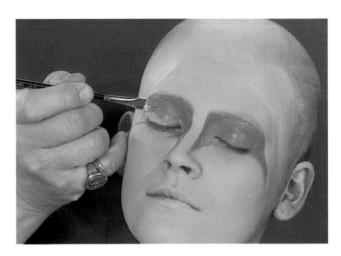

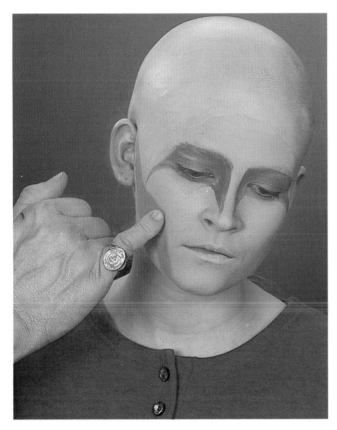

4 Decorate the cheeks with the same colours. Blend in the dry colours with your fingertips.

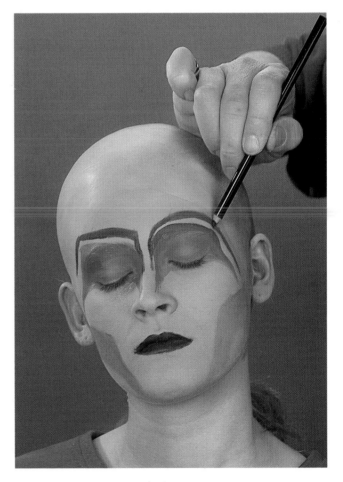

5 Paint the lips black and line the eyes with the eyebrow pencil. In a design like this, it is not necessary to make both sides of the face identical.

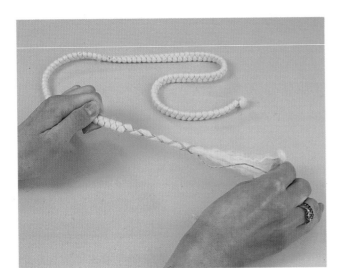

6 Now untie the length of crêpe hair.

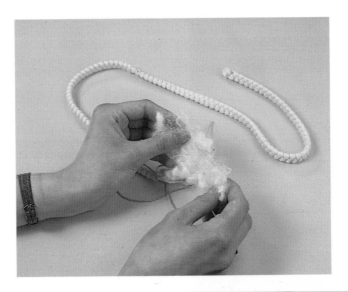

7 Make your length of hair fluffy by pulling and teasing it between your fingers.

8 Place the fluffed-out piece of hair on a sheet of newspaper. Colour with 'Kryolan' hairspray.

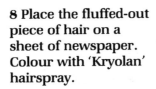

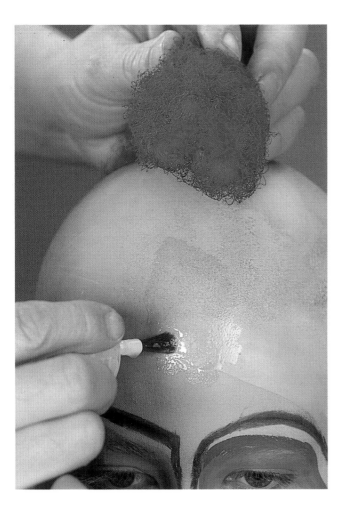

9 Put a line of spirit gum on the pre-impression cap and position the hair length on it.

10 The completed design. Compare this with the original sketch. Which of the four models was used for the punk?

Youth and age

You will need 'Aqua Colour'
shade 4W, a damp sponge,
rouge powder, a 1.2cm moppet
brush, sable brushes, brown,
highlight, ivory, carmine and
light-red 'Kryolan' colours,
an eyebrow pencil and a small
toothbrush.

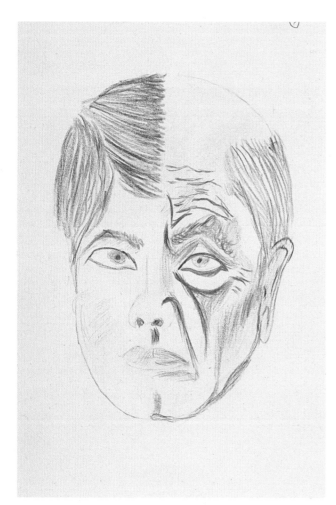

1 A sketch of the
design, showing how
one face can be made
to look both young
and old.

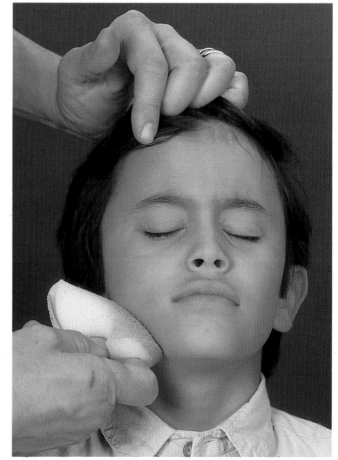

2 Give the whole face
a natural base colour
('Aqua Colour', shade
4W).

3 Begin on the side of the face which is to show youth. Apply rouge powder with the moppet brush to highlight the cheeks.

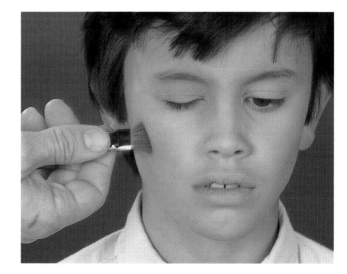

4 Emphasise the eyeline and eyebrow. Use brown 'Kryolan' for the eyeline and the eyebrow pencil for the eyebrow.

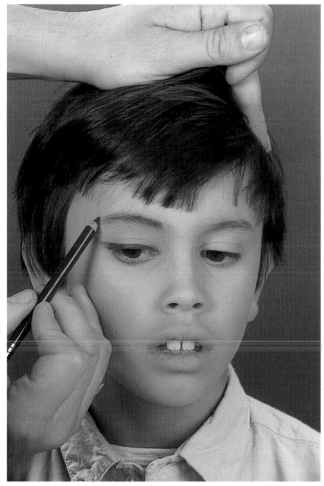

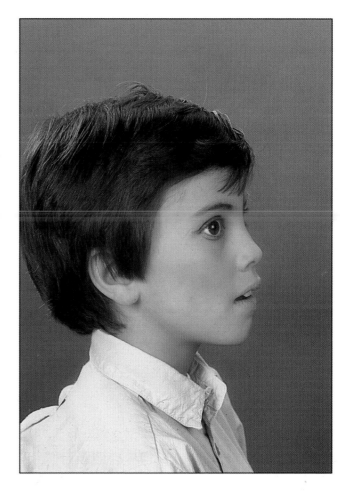

5 The young face.

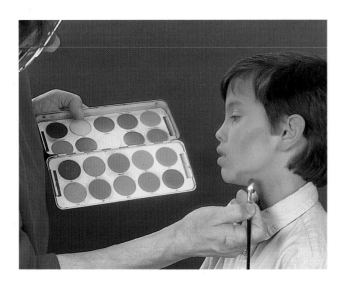

6 Now work on the side of the face which is to show age. Apply 'Kryolan' brown shadow-colour with a brush. Remember to darken the area beneath the cheekbone. Highlight the centre line of the nose, the nostril and the eyelid with highlight colour (applied in powder form).

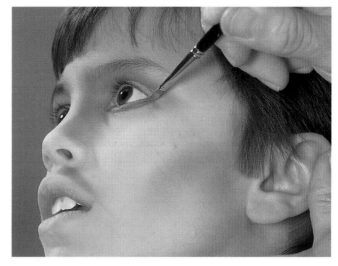

7 The eye will need to look red and baggy. Lines of carmine, light red and brown will achieve this effect.

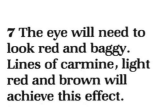

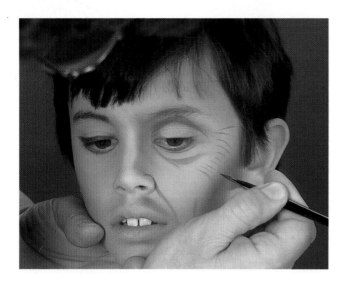

8 Add crease lines around the nose and mouth using brown 'Kryolan' applied by brush.

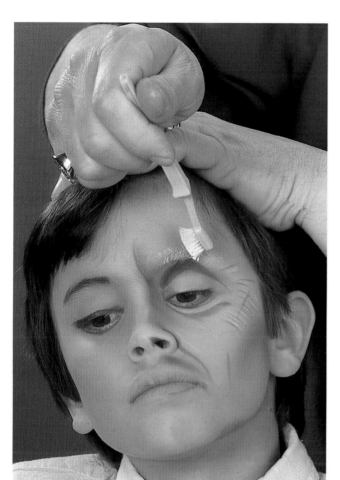

9 Make the eyebrow bushy by brushing it with ivory 'Kryolan' applied on the small toothbrush.

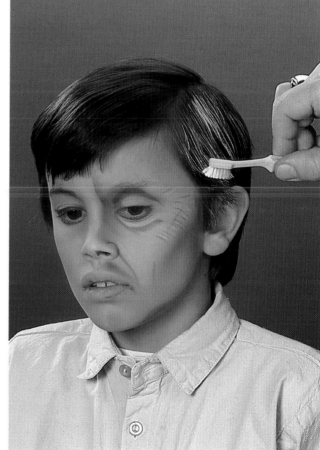

10 Ivory 'Kryolan' can also be used to make dark hair look old and grey. Ivory is always used for this because white looks blue under stage lights and on people with very dark hair.

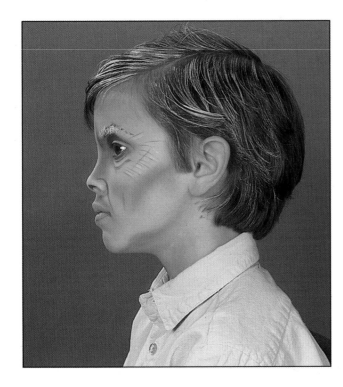

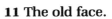

11 The old face.

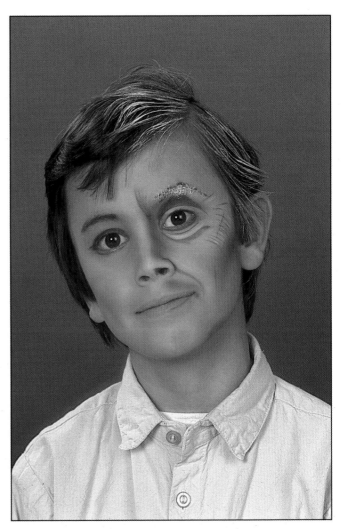

12 The completed design. Compare this with the original sketch.

You will need a pre-impression cap, spirit gum, sponges, white 'Aqua Colour', black and brick-red 'Kryolan' colours, a 1.2cm moppet brush and a sable brush (size 6).

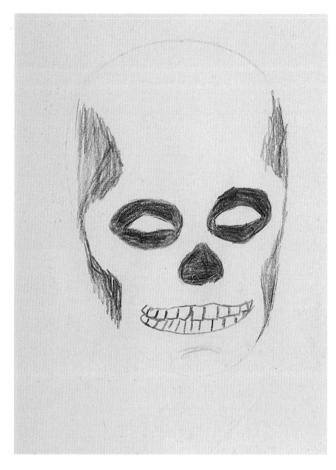

1 A sketch of the design.

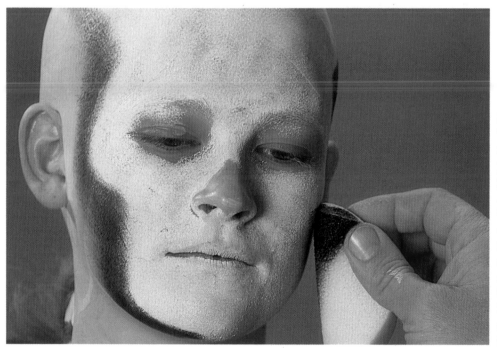

2 Cover the hair with the pre-impression cap and fix it in position with spirit gum. (See page 12.) Apply white 'Aqua Colour' over the cap and face, leaving the nose and eye areas clear. Add a shading of black 'Kryolan' to the white areas around the edge of the face to define the shape of the skull.

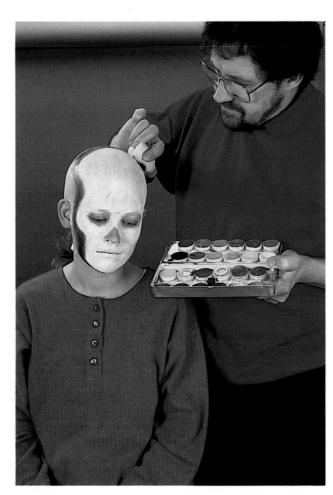

3 Mottle the white areas with brick red 'Kryolan'. Using a sponge, dab on the colour so that the white surface is made to look old and decayed.

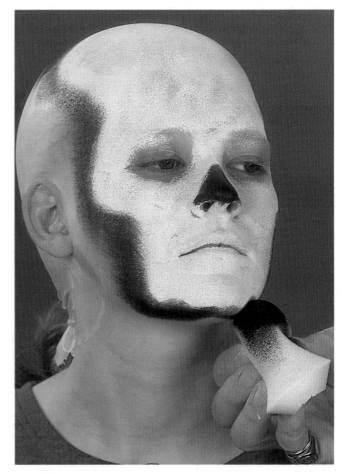

4 Black out the nose...

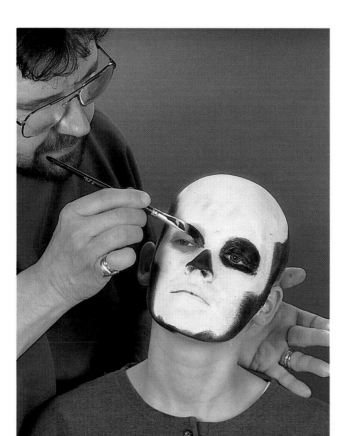

5 ... and, using the moppet brush, darken the eye sockets.

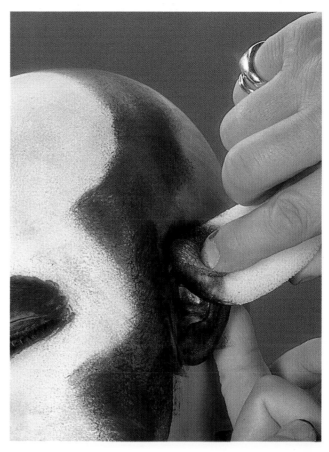

6 The ears will need to be blacked out too, or they can be left under the pre-impression cap.

7 Now paint the mouth line, using the sable brush, ...

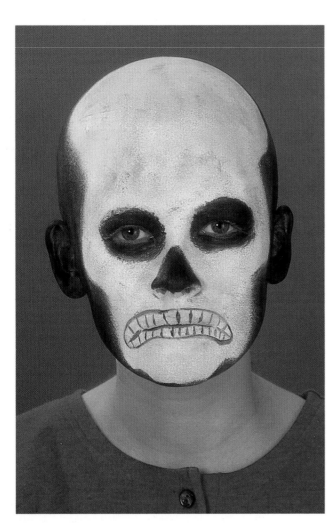

8 ... and add a broken line of teeth.

9 The completed design. Compare this with the original sketch.

You will need red, ginger, gold, pink and white 'Kryolan' colours, and a sable brush (Size 6).

1 A sketch of the design.

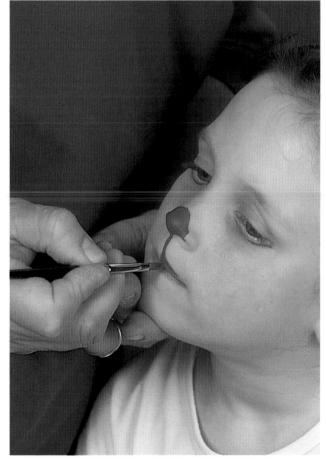

2 No base colour is required for this design. Begin with the nose, applying red 'Kryolan' with the sable brush. Notice that the nose line runs into the lips.

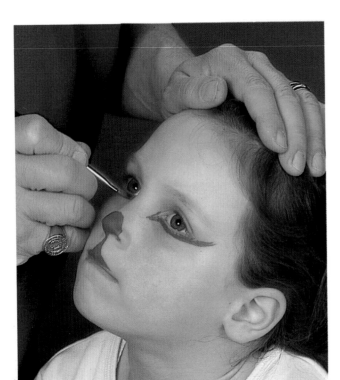

3 The eye shape must be that of an animal, not a human!

4 Lines above and below the eyes will help achieve this effect.

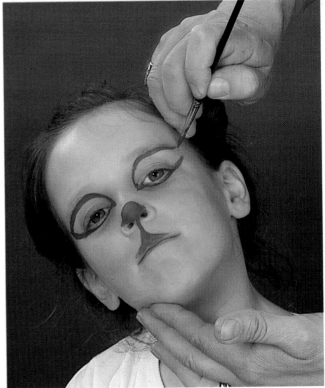

5 Begin to draw in the fur.

6 First texture the face with ginger lines then with lines of gold.

7 Finally add pink and white colour to the mouth line and to the eyelids.

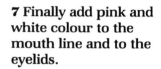

8 The completed design. Compare this with the original sketch and with the photograph of Amy on page 11.

You will need a pre-impression cap, spirit gum, a damp sponge, black, brown and white 'Kryolan' colours, brushes, and an eye pencil.

1 A sketch of the design.

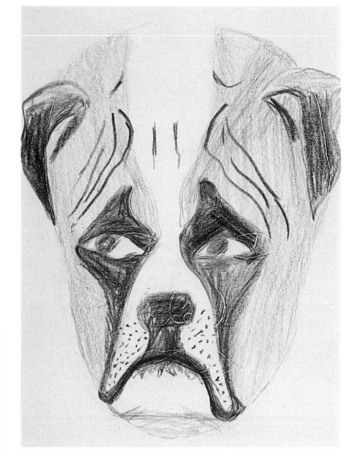

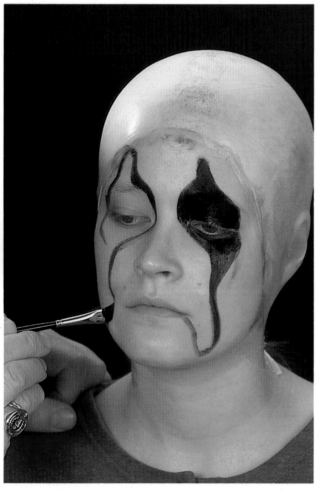

2 Cover the hair and ears with the pre-impression cap and fix it in position with spirit gum. (See page 12.) Colour the eyes with black 'Kryolan', extending the design above and below the eye sockets.

3 Now add detail to the nose...

4 ... and lips.

5 Colour the sides of the head with brown 'Kryolan'.

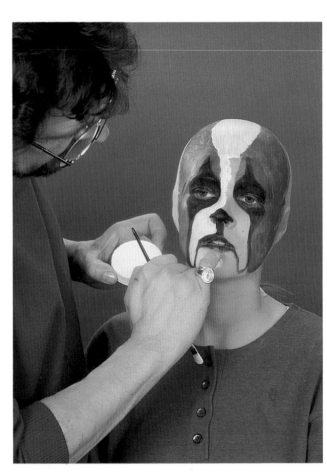

6 Use white 'Kryolan' to fill the areas which remain uncovered. Use the tip of a brush to sharpen and define the white edge.

7 Use the eye pencil for whiskers...

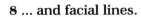
8 ... and facial lines.

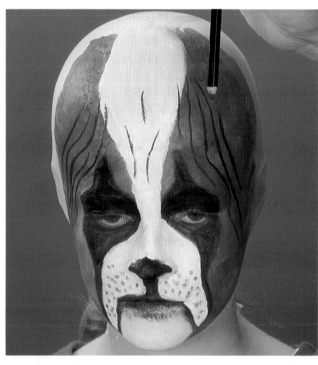

9 The completed design. Compare this with the original sketch and with the photograph of Emma on page 15.

Here are some other sketches
which you might like to use as
the basis for designs of your own.

1 *Old Lady.*

2 *The Duchess.*

3 *Spirit.*

4 *The Devil.*

5 A design in brick red.

Further information

Getting clean again

Water-based colours are as easy to remove as they are to apply.

Begin by softening any areas where spirit gum has been used, with spirit gum remover. Apply the remover on a piece of cotton wool. When the gum is soft, false hair (beards, moustaches) and the pre-impression cap can be gently eased away from the skin. If the skin remains a little sticky when the hair or cap has been removed, clean off any gum which remains with the remover.

The paint is removed by washing with soap and hot water. It is best to wash the face several times – using fresh water – drying it between washes on paper towels. Use a wad of cotton wool to clean around the ears and around the eyes and nose.

Finally, when your model looks clean, wash once more to make sure every trace of paint has disappeared! It is an unwritten rule that actors never leave the theatre with stage-make-up on.

Websites

United Kingdom

www.facepaintshop.co.uk
Everything you need for face painting

www.bodydeco.co.uk
More face-painting equipment

www.screenface.com
Shops in London and online supplies

www.3kmake-up.com
Theatrical make-up supplies

www.facepaintingdesigns.co.uk
Lots of new ideas for other face-painting designs in the online gallery

Australia

www.ashtonadmor.com.au
Suppliers of theatrical make-up

www.theartshop.com.au
Online art shop selling face paints

 **Index**